DARK MATTERS

Mantz Yorke

To David
with best wishes

Mantz

19.4.23

Dark Matters

© Mantz Yorke

First Edition 2021

Mantz Yorke has asserted his authorship and given his permission to Dempsey & Windle for these poems to be published here.

Published by Dempsey & Windle
15 Rosetrees
Guildford
Surrey
GU1 2HS
UK
01483 571164
dempseyandwindle.com

British Library Cataloguing-in-Publication Data

A catalogue record for this book is available from the British Library

ISBN: 978-1-013329-38=9

For Jon, Steve and Susie

Contents

The Sinkhole

Animosities live long in this unstable land
undermined by channels and caves,
where differences are bombastic and brutal –
teeth for teeth and eyes for eyes.

Kneeling, he looks down into the blackness,
past the ferns and beeches
grown like scrub in the twenty-seven years
since solid ground became a pit.
He scrolls through his pride at bearing a gun;
the men marching the captive
to the rim; the shot to the back of the head;
the bent body tumbling
into the blackness and the hidden river below;
the brotherhood celebrating
his initiation with spirits and the roasting of a goat;
and the morning after,
hung over, a raven's cark rasping in his ears.

Are twenty years with Médecins Sans Frontières
sufficient expiation?
No priest to answer or confer absolution:
only the shot,
the blackness, the unfading reverberation.

Reflections: The Vietnam Veterans' Memorial, Washington DC

You reached up
and pointed to the name
in the polished stone:
a paler you reached up
and touched your fingertips
with cold.

His name,
one of fifty-eight thousand,
three hundred and seven
graved into the black gabbro
is the nation's acknowledgement
of the gift of life.

You have known
for four decades and more
his life was no gift;
that indifferent politicians,
bombing, burning and shooting
in the name of freedom,
had asserted their inalienable right
to dispossess.

Tokens at the wall –
crosses, flowers, flags,
unwanted articles of war –
mark bereavements:
veterans have left scrawls,
unsigned, unaddressed,
whose confusion cries out

from this numbing
crescendo and diminuendo
of plutonic dark.

You see yourself among the dead,
unclearly,
through tears you cannot name.

The End of the Campaign

Solitudinem faciunt, pacem appellant
('They make a desert, and call it peace' — Calgacus, chronicled by Tacitus)

The drone's hi-res images
display the shape of the city –
its grid neatly rectangular,
save for the historic centre's
curlicues of roads –

but the houses and shops
are a vague rubble,
defined sporadically
by corners of masonry
untoppled by sudden shocks.

At first glance, the images
resemble the devastation
wreaked by a violent quake –
Bam's mud-brick buildings
collapsed by an unknown fault –

but pipes and steel rods
projecting out of concrete
and craters in the roads
tell of destruction by missiles,
mortars, shells and bombs.

It seems no-one is left alive.
On sand blackened by blood
bloated bodies are drawing flies;
now and then we glimpse a rat
scurrying in its hunt for food.

In desert combat kit,
we're on full alert, just in case
the rubble conceals an enemy
with a machine-gun
or an explosive vest.

But there's no resistance
after the long bombardment:
amid the devastation
we raise our flag, relax with a cig,
and congratulate ourselves

on a city at last at peace.

Liberation

The rendered walls are pockmarked;
some brickwork has been exposed;
shutters are closed, their louvres
eyelids drooping in naïve defence
against assault. Soldiers are advancing,
rifles at the ready, across rubble
created by mortar bombs and shells.

Where is this? Some unremarkable town
in France, Poland, Germany, Ukraine?
Which year? The picture's timelessness
hints at a condemnation: history
repeated as tragedy, and not as farce.

Betrayal

What loyalty made you leak material
declared classified or inappropriate
for all to know? Security necessitates
some silence, but what morality conceals

diplomacy sweetening deals with bribes,
contractors abusing human rights,
random shootings in a fury of revenge,
families blasted by misdirected bombs?

Your treatment on remand – 'cruel and unusual',
denied exercise, light, and sometimes clothes –
and a sentence as lengthy as a murderer's
suggest the Eighth Amendment no longer holds.

Your match lit up dark closets of the state,
but who is the betrayer; who is the betrayed?

The Eighth Amendment to the US Constitution prohibits the federal
government from imposing, *inter alia*, cruel and unusual punishments,
including torture.

War Game

The terrain tilts, swerves
on his console
as he manoeuvres
the distant drone.

He enters co-ordinates
for the target, the missile locks on,
then **ZAP!** In a flash,
mud bricks are rubble and dust.

The second, exploding
among scrabbling villagers,
completes the mission.
Game over.

Later, evaluators
send back news:
the incorrect co-ordinates
will be excused.

Bloody Monday, Derry

i.m. Brian Friel, and remembering a performance of 'The Freedom of the City' at the Abbey Theatre, Dublin

A bit of a lark,
the three arrivals from the street
making merry in the mayor's parlour,
drinking whiskey and sherry,
as protesters in Guildhall Square flee
water cannon, rubber bullets
and CS gas.

A megaphone
demands they lay down their arms
and leave. Hands up, trusting,
they emerge to an unlit stage,
save for spotlights on their faces,
till rifles crack
and all goes black.

In the shocking dark
there's time to dab tears away
before the living dead,
but not the Sunday dead,
beamingly revive and bow
to a huge explosion
of applause.

Tommy at Seventy

In appreciation of Harold Gillies' pioneering work with severely disfigured servicemen.

Three score an' ten.

           Yer'd not 'ave bet on it back then,
me stuck in Sidcup wi' bandages where shrapnel
took 'alf me face. I never saw me worst: the 'ospital
'id the mirrors so us in there couldn't see usselves,
but we knew what we was like – we'd see mates
wi' tubes of rolled-up flesh an' skin 'angin' down
an' pinned where they'd be stretched in place.

The doc told me me flesh 'd take months growin'
enough to cover me face. 'E was me cornerman,
'is kit better than Vaseline, styptic an' a sponge:
'e got me fit for fightin' the next round – doin'
ARP down the old East End.

           I ain't 'andsome
like I was, but I ain't come out too bad, blessed
wi' a lovely wife and two great kids who're proud
I did me bit.

           Me mates too 'ad done their bit:
the doc, 'e fixed 'em best as 'e could. Some stayed in;
some went 'ome but then just 'id, afraid o' bein'
gawped at wi' their patched-up looks. Most got nowt
for going through 'ell – no medals, nor an 'int o' fame –
but I'm tellin' yer, an' I'll bloody well tell yer again,
they was 'eroes all the same.

Resurrection: the Sandham Memorial Chapel, Burghclere

After Stanley Spencer's murals depicting his experience of World War 1

Released from graves, they dump redundant crosses
before the seated Christ. To their left, comrades
glance up from trenches towards this resurrection,
perhaps for the first time believing death is no more
than a rest on the winding ascent to heaven.

Elsewhere, a convoy bears wounded into hospital;
obsessively, a shell-shocked soldier scrubs the floor
and others, under mosquito nets, are being told
the war that was supposed to end all wars
is over, and they can anticipate returning home.

You might imagine resurrection would pass down
a legacy of experience and understanding,
and that emergent souls would have encouraged us
to defy those who've assumed control and demand
we beat our ploughshares into swords.

The risen would be dismayed that their brief lives
have not prevented further inscriptions on the scroll
of inhumanity – Guernica, London, Stalingrad, Dresden,
Hiroshima, Grozny, Srebrenica, Baghdad, Gaza, Aleppo,
along with terrorism and agencies' black ops.

There's no New Jerusalem waiting to descend.
Only when we've stopped the bullets, the shells,
the bombs, the gas, can we ourselves construct it
from the rubble scattered across those graveyards
where poppies alone retain the nerve to bloom.

Poppies

Coils of rusty bramble define the boundaries of soil
November rain has darkened like blood. Heeled
deep down in the ploughman's ruts, the tiny seeds lie
shrouded in black and dormant, far from the sway
of empty censers. A drab landscape huddles in the cold.

Late in their season, pale shoots escape the strangle
of roots. Uncrumpling, survivors flutter scarlet
in the flurries rippling through ranks of corn
withering in the summer heat. Pollen drifts
in the fitful breeze, like cordite over a foreign field.

At the Cenotaph, London

Big Ben clangs
the eleventh hour
of the eleventh day,
of the eleventh month.
We fall silent,

remembering.

Leaders wait
in thick black coats
and medalled uniforms
for the Last Post
to call them
to the laying-down
of wreaths.

Time freezes.

At attention,
they gaze beyond
the Cenotaph
seeing ghosts
receding
into the fog:

they do not see,
behind,
more spectres
advancing,
a column
without end.

Stilled

After 'Filter', a sculpture in Manchester City Art Gallery, UK, featuring Antony Gormley's body, and Richard Drew's photograph 'The Falling Man'.

Exoskeleton of steel rings   That 9/11 photograph

black against a white wall   a man falling head down
the body is suspended   on the terminator
arrested mid-fall   between light and dark

stilled

in space   in time

immortal

Awayday

Evening. The sea far out.
Runnels between the sandbanks,
traps for the incautious
each time the tide slinks back.
Above the groynes,
a lone family, huddled
against the wind, watches a kite –
a silhouette in the low sun –
haul a buggy across the sand.

*

That hot summer afternoon
no one bothered about the lads
half a mile away, kicking a ball
at the margin of a sea
they thought unthreatening.

And when the sea slid in,
suddenly too deep for them
to wade, too chill to swim,
no one heard their shouts
above the beach-buzz
and the wavelets' shushing
as they died.

Hawthorns, Wastwater

About thirty-five degrees – scree's
natural angle, judging by the map:
you'd believe it more, looking up

the exaggerated perspective of the fan
to its origin and vanishing-point,
where the roaring wind is flattening mist
against gullies and splintered crags.

The path winds its impermanent way
around stony convexities,
contouring roughly around the lake.

Here and there, set against the slants
of green, rust and clinkery black,
hawthorns writhe and cringe,
offering up blood-red fruits

as if to propitiate the rain,
their life-span determined
by a random tumbling-down of stones.

Khao Lak, Thailand, Boxing Day 2004

From my Olympian height, the beach,
no longer just a fringe to tropical lush,
is a vast expanse of sand swept smooth
between rocks normally submerged.

I shout as loudly as I can to the solitary man
staring out to sea, for I have seen
what he yet has not – the humungous
foaming combers sweeping back to reclaim
what had been yielded up, and more.

Far below, he cannot hear: too late,
he understands what's coming,
turns back, and disappears.

Mayflies

Unhurried, the river
lacks the impetus of rain.
I sit on a bank
lined by alders:
mayflies are dancing
in the shafts of sun.

A flick in a dappled pool
held by a root:
the brown trout
betrays its camouflage
as it too waits.
Death is closing in.

Hag Stone

i.m. Keith Collins

Waves are easing pebbles
        along the beach,
weeds are encroaching
        on the shingle,
rails, cables and winches
        are rusting,
abandoned hulls
        are rotting,
cod are moving north,
        escaping
the English Channel's
        increasing warmth.

Day to day, the changes
        are imperceptible
even though you know
        they're happening.
Now and then abruptness
        compels your attention,
like a fisherman's hut
        blown flat by a storm,
or an X-ray image exposing
        headaches as malign.

You gave me a hag stone
        on a loop of garden twine
(to bring me luck, you said)
        but, unwittingly,
you gave away the luck
        you really should have kept.

River Wye, Monsal Dale

i.m. Mike Daniel

Shadowed water, in places
so dark you hardly notice
the gently weaving weed.

A stark ridge, sharp
against the sky, wavers
where the flow anticipates

the fisherman's dam.
A jet's bright filament,
snaking and whorling

across the sky's deep
reflected blue, reaches
the plunge, and is cut.

At the Hospice Window

She's shrunken now, her body too small
for her clothes. Each day she lists the birds
she's seen at the feeder – always a flutter
of sparrows and tits, occasionally a robin
bossing its territory and blackbirds scuffling
underneath, scavenging for fallen seeds.

Today she was radiant, excited, the lines
on her face less deep. A charm of goldfinches
had been tussling for perches on the mesh,
her book's photograph made live. 'You know
what the birds signify?' I shook my head.
She smiled. 'Resurrection', she said.

Friar's Crag, Derwentwater

This is their time – low season in the Lakes,
between summer and the half-term break.
In comfortable clothes, they pick their way
across the cracked crag's varicose roots
to the lakeside seats (a repetition in slo-mo
of their more snappily-fashioned spring).

Kittenish paws dab playfully, ruffling
the glassy lake while the sun, sinking
on Causey Pike, burns the first-turning oaks.
Nearby, a branch, its leaves sepia-crisp, rests
on a fungussy stump, and birches' yellow
sequins are shivering as if anticipating frost.

This is their time: not ready yet to move on,
they'll sit until the sun's last sliver is gone.

Shuffling Homeward

A dull October day. Rain
begins to fall from clouds
grey as the shadows
that give substance to our being.
Here the freshly-fallen leaves –
yellow, red and orange – hush
the feet of mourners leaving
the dead: the dying
fires of autumn linger
over the graves,
scattering ashes in the guttering
light of late afternoon.

The dampness of decay
rises as we shuffle homeward
through the leaves – past ebullience
turned dank and mouldering,
awaiting the cleanliness of frost.
Soon clocks will be turned back,
evenings draw in quicker
than ever we expect:
shall we be prepared?
Have we candles to light
the journey we will one day make
down this same pathway?

The Scattering

Swinging the kissing gate at the wood's edge, I remember
my childhood terror as *The Jungle Book*'s Nagaina uncoiled

and slithered silently under a bramble-sprawl. The grass snake
would be the frightened one today: the spaniels are boisterous,
excitedly following scents and snagging twigs in their coats
while a cold wind tests the leaves' hold on hawthorns, cherries,
sweet chestnuts and sycamores. Underfoot, the reddish earth

is splattered with the fall – yellows, ochres, browns
and the sweet chestnuts' urchiny green. Beyond the wood, sun
pierces the raggy cloud, highlighting, unexpectedly white
against a patch of grey, the spire of the parish church
amongst whose shaded gravestones I once believed I'd lie.

Time to do what we have gathered for. I uncap the square,
squat polythene flask that still surprises me with its weight,
and scatter the first granules of calcined bone: a chemistry
slower than the mermaid's will dissolve these ashes, allowing
rain and gradient to ease their atoms imperceptibly to the sea.

The others take their turns at scattering, leaving me to remember
the last time I saw her, dressed in vivid, non-octogenarian pink,
her stump supported by a stool, and talking animatedly
about the future and how she'd cope. At home later, the phone
ringing; my sister telling of her sudden collapse and death.

Obsequies done, we disperse. Dark curtains are drawing across
the dying afternoon; beneath them, parallelograms of rain.

Arnside Knott

The lane disappoints. Last year, cascades of blackberries
ripe for picking: today, most are tight-fisted green,
the crop perhaps three weeks short of its peak.
The road to the Knott yields only scrawny fruit –
less than a pound in my box, against last year's six.

I climb to the top of the rock-strewn slope, stopping at the trees
where we scattered ashes. Little time for remembrance, though:
rain's grey drapes are closing on Morecambe Bay. I descend
a harebelled field, exchanging wary looks with Highland cows –
this time, there's no white bell striking amid the blue.

The rail-fare's been poor value as far as blackberrying goes,
but there've been compensations: a hedge's mauve-hazed sloes,
peacocks on knapweed's magenta tufts, meadow browns
flittering between bushes on the limestone screes,
robin's pincushions burning amongst barbs of rose.

We're told a couple of hours exercising each week
will keep us fit: this walk has been better than going to a gym,
pedalling vigorously on a bike, and getting nowhere fast.

West Kennet Long Barrow

After van Gogh's 'Wheatfield with Crows'

Van Gogh would have been seduced
into painting this landscape – thundery
clouds against the tawniness of barley
close to harvesting, the random green
of unripened ears, and the bristly awns
kids set crawling up their shirted arms.
He might have added a straggle of crows
as a nod to those whose arthritic bones,
interred in this hilltop tomb, became
grist for medicines five centuries ago.

Once a barrier, sarsens merely pretend
the barrow's defence: a narrow gap
allows us to enter burial chambers
dimly lit by sky. Nothing there now
but desiccated herbs – the residue
of midsummer joyfulness or, perhaps,
tributes to the long-departed dead.

Heritage, Porth y Nant, North Wales

Propped by its flue, the building's slump-shouldered end
headstones a grave whose rubbled boundary has been smoothed
by time and grass. Rain has eroded its upper-circle yard: rusted,
a winch is poised to join the detritus scattered across the pebbles
fringing the sea. Down on the beach, where winter breakers
have battered the jetty to a solitary stump and smashed

the plugs of a half-buried V-8 back to its corroded block,
rocker-box tops shine like silver razor-shells. The sea today
is a slow surge stumbling on the shore, scuffing up the shingle
as it scrambles to its feet. Unmotivated to further violence,
it seems content to leave disintegration to the inexorable
thermodynamics of bacteria, mould, oxygen and salty spray.

A century ago quarrymen sledged gimlets into the cliffs,
tamped powder into the holes, sheltered from the blast, chiselled
the riven granite, and loaded wagons hauled high on dipperish rails.
The brambled galleries were then benches in a brumy amphitheatre –
its stage the sea, the players smutty coasters bringing exotica
from Liverpool and returning with setts to pave the ways for more.

The morning air is still, undusty. Above the quarry and caulish sea
the only sound is the whish-whish of a passing raven's wings.
Resin is diffusing from a stand of spruce, overpowering
the smell from supermarket bags of rotting scraps. Abandoned,
a steel toolbox of spanners, screwdrivers and sockets
is a casual gauge for the rain that is slowly turning them to rust.

Sett: a square paving stone

The Red Dancers

After Robert Macfarlane's trek from Å to Kollhellaren

Fresh snow. No sound
bar the squeak of boots.
The invisible path
between threats
of avalanche and gully-fall
steepening, demanding
crampons on, helmet on,
ice-axe in hand and ready
to chop through
the corniced crest. Above,

the sea eagle
circling, circling, circling.

The sea's margin:
hours scrambling across
boulders, scrub, crags
to the settlement
below the rock face,
now merely a ground-plan
laid out in stones.
Beyond, the maelstrom –
not, as Poe imagined,
a glassy moulin swirling
to the underworld –
merely choppy water
and a galaxy of foam.

And above, the sea eagle
circling, circling, circling.

In the cave, gloom,
a hint of grey daylight.
They must be here; surely
they've survived,
those rusty stick-figures
drawn millennia ago
to welcome arrivals
into the world below.
Look. Look harder.
Look harder still... There!
And in streaming eyes
they're dancing, dancing.

Outside, the sea eagle
circling, circling, circling.

Ascension Day

Feral shadows prowl beyond
the flickering fire:
fear-filled eyes gleam back
a power unrealised.

I sense fulfilment as I watch
candescent prophets turn to ash,
whirlwinds sear the city streets,
sucking air from screaming lungs
while tongues caress
the buildings' wounds.

I am
Lord of the Earth
ascended from the algal slime
to claim the throne that's rightly mine.

I ride my red horse,
nostrils aflame,
breathing life to the pyre
built on the dark plain,
cremating the water,
the earth and the air:
in the embers of dawn,
pale is his hair.

Ant-hills now shiver
at the shock of his feet;
frantic, the living
flee from the light,
burying their futures
in collapsing sand
as the Second Law clutches
the shuddering land.

No sanctuary in the crumbling church
where peeling icons hear no prayers.
The King is dead! Long live the King!
Unbelievers, kiss my ring!
The present and the past are dead:
only chaos lies ahead.

These feet can't tread out the nitred line
drawn to the coronation feast
unwitting souls prepared to toast
the radiant dawning of my reign.

Critical Incident, 21 May 1946

You assembled the core for Trinity –
that first atomic bomb burst in the desert –
and had been awarded lapel pins
because you'd helped open the doors
for Little Boy to fall on Hiroshima
and Fat Man on Nagasaki.

Nicknamed *chief armorer of the US*
for your expertise in constructing bombs,
you carried on experimenting
('tickling the dragon's tail', colleagues said),
easing hollow half-spheres of beryllium
around a plutonium core
so reflected neutrons could edge fission
towards criticality – a risky procedure,
riskier still when you used a screwdriver
instead of the customary shims
to keep the beryllium shells apart.

The screwdriver slipped:
the beryllium bivalve clammed shut,
a chain reaction ran amok,
and the watchers' eyes filled for a moment
with blue light. Straightaway
you wrenched the shells apart – too late
to prevent the burst of radiation
giving you three-dimensional sunburn
and silently pronouncing sentence
on your recklessness: life,
to be served for a mere nine days.

Louis Slotin died on 30 May 1946 from the radiation released in this
accident.

Fallout

Spectacular, the thundercloud drifting out to sea,
a tiara of crepuscular rays on its softly-anvilled top.

Back then, we didn't appreciate the insidiousness of rain
dripping into the earth the fallout from atomic tests –
strontium-90, a ready substitute for calcium in bones,
and caesium-137, as absorbable as salt.

Their buckshot of beta-particles, unfelt, damaged
flesh and bone beyond repair – a necessary price
(not paid by governments) for protecting all of us
from nuclear war. We've long known the risks

of atmospheric bursts, and nations' self-denial still holds,
but all is not well. Windscale, Three Mile Island,
Chernobyl and Fukushima have reminded us
treaties won't shield us from unstable atoms' power:

we rightly fear the legacy of the choices made for us –
the blanching of our blood, our flesh consumed by crabs.

Dreamcatcher

The T-shaped frame stands proud
of the shingle. On suspended spindles,
prisms of white cloth are swinging
to the whim of the wind. *Why?* I wonder.

Home, the web tells me
the cloth, downwind of Dungeness B,
is there to trap bits of radioactivity –
a catcher of nightmares

but giving no protection
to those who live there,
unlike the charmed webs protecting
the first Americans from harm.

The Blossoming, Kopelovo, 1986

In the orchard, the breaking
of pinkish buds. The horizon,
once distant through winter twigs,
has drawn in, a stippled ring
of green and apple-white. Light

is falling through the branches
of a chestnut, dappling shadows
on a grey-green tent and the patient
queue shuffling forward in the hot
pollen-dusty air. Here

white-coated orderlies welcome us
with curious words, microphones
crackle like radio static
and syringes gorge themselves
on our blood. All is well,

they tell us; we'll go home soon,
when the petals are lying white
upon the ground. We can't yet tell
the wind-blown pollen's struck,
and fruits have begun to swell.

Muslyumovo

1952

Sunlight dazzling from the white:
I'm lying by my upturned sledge, again
hearing my friends shriek as they skate
round the freezing bodies of men
squatting at holes in the ice. The heat
in the river bed is buried under cold.

We were told there was a city up-river
where elegant houses lined wide streets
and people ate chocolate. No children
came downstream to play with us.
No one came. Spring brought only slabs of ice
undulating and crunching on the silty flow.

That summer we splashed in the shallows,
shouting as water swooshed at us
from the flat slap of hands. We paddled,
then half-swam, a foot in the soft silt
enough to keep us afloat. On the bank
we daubed ourselves with mud, and baked.

1992

Autumn: each day longer than the last.
I am numb, save when the pain
spikes through the morphine. My eyes
cannot bear the glare of the white sheets
and the white wall, and on that wall
the rising shadow of mullion and transom.

Muslyumovo is a township near the Techa River, downstream from the
Mayak nuclear fuel reprocessing plant.

43

Dark Matter

They're enhancing the equipment:
he's enjoying the free day
sauntering round the abbey, admiring
columns and lancet windows
that seem as if a theme from Thomas Tallis,
anticipated in stone,
is reaching for the blue June sky.
He ponders the monks' commitment
to a Lord they could never see
but whose existence they inferred
from the beauty around them –
the glory of a sunrise,
a rainbow's brilliance,
berries in the hedgerow,
the hover of a kestrel,
the tracery of ice on glass.
He'd learned from science
not to twist conclusions
by selecting observations:
gazing at the ruins, he wonders
how the monks could have squared
the core of their belief
with squalor, hunger and disease.

Half a mile beneath the grass,
salt insulates the detector
from extraneous radiation.
He sits at the computer, hoping
the instrument's augmented sensitivity
will allow him to confirm
what mathematical analysis
has hypothesised – that dark matter
bulks out the universe.
Experience has taught him patience:
elsewhere, others underground
have, like him, yet to see
traces of the particles
scientists have convinced themselves exist.
Like Vladimir and Estragon,
they spend their burrowed time
waiting, waiting, waiting, waiting …

Climbing the Cuillin Ridge

To the Skye Mountain Rescue Team and the RAF Search and Rescue Team.

Ascent

Just what I came for – a glorious early morning, blue sky
with just a few wisps of cirrus in the west; the sun
warming the Black Cuillin while draping a grey cape
over the shoulders of Marsco and Glamaig. My last day
away from London: soon I'll be back in the humdrum
job in the laboratories – but this is joy, climbing sweatily
in T-shirt and shorts up the grassy slope of Fionn Choire
towards the bleak, black, jagged Cuillin ridge.

Above Harta Corrie, landmarks are disappearing
into mist; Loch Scavaig and Loch Coruisk have gone;
and here a compass needle can't be trusted. Rain
has driven in faster than I'd believed possible, draining
warmth from my shivering frame. Time to descend,
and quickly. No downward path visible: I take a gully
down into the corrie, knowing there'll be a long tramp
back past the Bloody Stone to Sligachan. It's steep,
slippery and, part-way down, blocked by a chockstone.
I squeeze round, but numb hands lose their grip and I fall,
boulders rising slowly, inexorably, to my unaverted face ...
Andromeda whirling ... supernovae bursting ... black.

Aftermath

He smiled at me from the wall, a wide, fledgling's grin
belying his forty years. 'Have you seen this man?'
the notice asked: just arrived, of course I'd not. On leaving,
though naturally I'd looked out, the same. So, too, the police
who, told he'd left possessions in his room a week ago,
wondered if he'd gone swimming in the loch, only to cramp
and drown unseen. So, too, the rescue team with their dogs,
who'd scoured the crags and gullies to no avail. A long month
till a helicopter crew, searching for another, chanced on him
in the outwash and radioed for help to bring him in.

A decade ago, I'd climbed the shattered slabs to the peak
of Bruach na Frithe, delighting in the lochs stretching hazily below.
Something I haven't the breath for now, so these days I ascend
in my imagination, plotting journeys over the contours
to Am Basteir, Sgurr Alasdair and the rest, always to that friable,
fissured edge – the height that sharply separates existence
from extinction. I imagine the exhilaration he must have felt
climbing those far Cuillins, before a flick of the jet stream
whisked him, like Mallory, Irvine and many more, into the void.

Incineration

The meadow grass is shrivelling, turning black:
the fiery ring is spreading, its heat burning deep
into my skin. I step back from the blaze,
acrid smoke stinging my eyes, and weep.

The tree stood at the centre of the field
we flew our kites in, its leafy cumulus
a shelter whenever it rained.
Nails in the trunk let us climb
beyond the hole my grandad showed me
(he said it was a woodpecker's,
but we never found an egg,
nor even the beginnings of a nest)
and on into the high branches
caressing the blue of a summer sky.
Swaying in the wind, we'd spread our sails
and bear towards New England,
whose autumn hues and teeming seas
lived on beyond each nightfall
and descent to sleep.

A livid cloud is spreading above a pillar of smoke.
Log by rotten log, the tree is crumbling into ash.
Far to the east a cold dead moon is rising, huge,
shivering in the superheated air.

Buzz Aldrin Celebrates Holy Communion, Tranquility Base

Before the door of Eagle was opened on the Sea of Tranquility, Buzz Aldrin (in civilian life an elder at Webster Presbyterian Church) celebrated Holy Communion whilst Neil Armstrong quietly looked on.

Relief,

    after they'd survived a descent to the surface
made riskier as Eagle missed the intended landing site,
their computer crashed, and fuel ran desperately low.

Silence.

    In weak gravity the communion wine swirls slowly, gracefully
into the chalice. Aldrin eats the wafer he'd brought, drinks,
and reads again the psalm's words he'd written on a card.

Meditation...

    His turn to exit. Under star-speckled black
he steps down the ladder to the surface grit
and into the unfiltered glory of the sun.

Reek Sunday, Croagh Patrick

A painful rallentando,
his pilgrimage – barefoot on quartzite adzes
sharp as the knives
Andersen's mermaid opted to tread.

He rests raw feet.
The sun, sliding towards a crest that's clear
one moment, gone the next,
urges him onwards, sure in his belief

he'll make it to the peak,
glory will fill his eyes, the chapel will be gold
and welcoming –
not cloistered by mist, its door firmly closed.

Croagh Patrick (nicknamed 'The Reek') is a mountain in County Mayo, Ireland.
On the last Sunday of July ('Reek Sunday') there is an annual pilgrimage to the
chapel on the summit.

Bray Head

There are two paths. Three nuns in jackdaw greys
have chosen the right, up concrete steps
and through the gorse clumps, towards a cross
that's clear-cut against the lowering sky.
I choose the gentler, muddier left, and meander

along the cliffs, unable to see the destination
of the railway below, but drawn on by spring's
indiscriminate strew – bluebells, stitchwort,
valerian and vetch, the treasury of pennywort
clinging to the stone, and always the promise

implicit in the next jut of rock. At the fork, signs
warned of weakening bridges: decades back,
this path was much more than a stroller's trail,
but now there's only a hint of past importance –
an ivy'd ruin, with a clump of nettles discouraging

close inspection. Further on, I see the whitish
slabbiness of buildings – an amorphous huddle
where aeons ago slate and sandstone yielded
to the soothing caress of time. Without a map,
I can't identify the town – maybe Greystones:

no matter, since I'll not get there and, anyway, rain
again is moving in. A brisk walk returns me
to the paths' divide. The nuns too are back,
bending to gather posies of bracken-crooks,
the cross above them now veiled by cloud.

St Martin's Church, Cwmyoy

Beyond the transept, the chancel, angled off,
signifies Christ crucified, sagged sideways
after commending his spirit to the Lord.
'Religion petrified' was Goethe's gloss
on gothic architecture: standing in the nave,
his dictum seems inappropriate for a church
lurching as if a typhoon's mountainous seas
had twisted its hull from end to end, listing
chancel to the south, tower to the north.

Early on, the landslide's shattered ground
exposed the foundations' frailty – walls
tilting and cracking as the earth yielded
to the stonework's weight. For now, buttresses
and rods driven into the walls have secured,
more than centuries of patchworked repairs,
the structure's wonky integrity against collapse,
though the bells of this 'crookedest church'
can no longer summon the faithful to attend.

Revelation, Church of St Mary the Virgin, Capel-y-ffin

Behind the altar-print of Christ, the panes
depicting bible scenes are now showing
nothing but overcast and the bare branches
of an ash. Last time I entered this simple church
the vivid orange of the casually-assumed
stained glass had begun a transformation,
revealing coloured paper curling at the edges
from condensation and the trespassing of rain.

Three o'clock. The hidden sun is subsiding
into wintry oblivion: time to move on. I leave
a pocket's small change in the collection box,
pass by the tilted headstones and ancient yews,
then climb a hillside path to find an oaken gate,
grey and sinewy as a puritan, with barbed wire
barring further progress. The nearby haw's
thorny crown is spattered with venous blood.

Graveyard, Church of St Mary the Virgin, Capel-y-ffin

Outside the whitewashed church, gravestones lean
towards each other, as if there's been subsidence
deep in the soil. An age of rain and frost
has flaked away some names: the Watkins'

decaying triptych has lost a son, yet remembers Sarah –
James' and Mary's girl – whose ten weeks breathing
the heavy, may-sweet air are no more than an artist's dot
in an infinite design. An inscription, half-hidden

by sorrel's folded leaves, acknowledges acceptance –
THE LORD GAVE AND THE LORD HATH TAKEN AWAY:
BLESSED BE THE NAME OF THE LORD. Rising from my knees,
I contemplate a valley enclosed by hills and unaware

of Nietzsche and the fragmentation of all that is.
A spatter heralds a cold front: soon the yew's acid drip
will renew its slow eroding of the sandstone,
grain by grain, that we may build from what is gone.

Quadratura, Sant'Ignazio, Rome

After Andrea Pozzo's trompe l'oeil *ceiling*

Inside the church, I obeyed the guide's injunction
not to raise my eyes until he said. Now looking
upwards I see, built four-square above the nave,
further storeys open to the skies, whose soft-lit columns
stretch towards the infinite. In this vast space Christ

floats above mundane architecture, drawing Ignatius
towards a paradise beyond the clouds. At my side
the guide is whispering how a strict geometry
of eyelines and a graticule of threads helped Pozzo
construct this illusion of the divine. I cannot remain,

unmoved by rapture: each step to the periphery reveals
the columns curling over me like pallid fingers
of a corpse, and the unboundedness of space
constrained by paint. I admire the determination
of this artifice, then slip out into the piazza's blaze.

Nativity, St Ives

Below the parish church, he and she –
grey slate bodies, granite oval heads –
face each other on a foreshore slab:
between their chests, a pinkish stone
shaped like a heart. In front of them,
the infant sleeping on a brick-like rock
is a whitish pebble and a sliver of slate.

This simple scene charms visitors
walking the sea wall: some chute coins
to the man in a dark blue shirt, jeans
and a cowboy hat who's now balancing
cobbles on cobbles, end on end,
ringing the tableau with statuary
as lasting as wind and tide will allow.

Regeneration

A few walls, garishly stuccoed, stand windowless
above the concrete slabs, bricks and splintered wood
strewn haphazardly as if a tornado had touched down.
They'll soon finish the destruction of our tenements:
in the distance a solitary white house keels over
like an iceberg top-heavied by the warmth of the sea.

Bulldozers are clambering jerkily over the rubble,
scooping and levelling, readying the ground
for the stadium and apartments we've been assured
will bring investment and jobs. From our hillside
shacks we gaze over the detritus of our homes
towards a downtown goldened by the shafting sun.

Town

This was once my home.

The weathered sandstone market-place
still shelters trade in bric-à-brac, secondhand
paperbacks and the produce of local farms,
and a few long-established names remain
along the streets. But much has gone:

the grocer's that smelt of rindy cheese,
with its bacon-slicer, bins of flour, and sugar
scooped into dark blue bags; the cinema
where we watched cowboys through the haze
rising from our fags; and the brewery
wafting the smell of malting barley
through unshuttered windows' mesh.

Now shops on the brewery land sell ice creams,
souvenirs, greeting cards and pre-packed food.
Nearby, dealers in antiques extract brass
ornaments and furniture from country homes,
promising rapid carriage to London and the States.
Off the Brampton Road the hollow's rivulet
has been dammed and its winding line of trees
lopped down to open out the view. I cried here

once, when my sister put into her mouth
nightshade berries from the rambunctious hedge
and was made to spit them out. Today she and I
walk through the reddish potato-furrowed field
where I used to scrump strawberries, disparaging
the concrete shed that so grossly parodies
the contour of Penyard Chase. Above the town

the parish church, its crumbling pinnacles
expensively restored, still stabs towards the blue
spring sky. As a child I never questioned
ending among its gravestones high above the Wye,
but I realise I won't belong there now:

this is not my town.

Draughts

The pieces have been placed.
A black piece is advanced
diagonally,
matched by a white.

Belatedly, the players realise
they've failed
to set out the board
as it should have been:

the black pieces
are on black squares,
the white on white,
unable to engage.

They reset the board,
start anew.

A Woman of Consequence

In appreciation of the legacy of Henrietta Lacks

In her small town she'd never have imagined
a court ruling her 'discarded tissue and cells'
were grist for commerce and no longer hers,
or the huge tonnage replicated from her legacy,
or the register of patents from medical research.
I'd like to believe she's looking down, happy
that the cancer cells taken from her body
had been cultured to immortality, gifting
science the chance to experiment with cures.

You mail samples for testing, seeking details
of your ancestries, but you've not realised –
like those who skip small print on contracts –
the full implications of what you've done.
Your DNA, like Henrietta's cells, has value:
you've licensed companies that search
for missing fragments of family filigree
to profit from your disclosures, and serve
merely collaterally your personal good.

Discounted

Twenty per cent off women's clothing:
who could resist?

I stand outside the fitting rooms, looking around
whilst she decides.

Nearby, black dummies dressed in orange,
ochre and olive

look magnificent: on real women, the clothes
would knock you out.

I look to see how many black women are here:
not a single one walks past.

Helen Bradley's Autumn

Panicles like candy floss hung on
longer than smoke,
became miniature tumbleweeds
rolling round the garden.
The cotinus' leaves, unexceptional
all summer, held fire
till autumn's chilly evenings drew in
their chlorophyll
and the oval whorls could disclose
the latency of flame.

Beginning with Miss Carter (in pink,
like the smoke bush),
Helen painted for her grandchildren
childhood recollections
of family, Mr Taylor and the dogs,
resuming the career
abandoned at fifteen, to find herself
surprised by the delight
folk took in her joyful picturings
of a Lancashire long gone.

Sic Transit

Shadows stretch from the autumnal sun
towards the small businesses and low-rise offices
where foundries once belched a breathtaking smoke.
We sit in his front garden: he is dozing in his wheelchair,
wrapped in a blanket despite the warmth of the air,
a translucent tube feeding his gritted lungs.

He wakes, looks down on the valley where he worked,
begins all over again...

I were tellin' yer me nan –
she were fourth o' the five that made it –
lived in Pitt Street in a two up, two down,
wi' mould-black walls just one brick thick.
No water in the houses then, she said:
folk drew it from the courtyard pump –
but courtyard is too fancy a word
for a shared area fringed with wash-houses
and privies whose stink never blew away.

Her dad 'd leave the murk each day
to trudge up to the mill – that was
till McKinley's tax on woollen goods
gave the boss just the opportunity
to demand the workers accepted wages
that were more realistic, or else
they'd find themselves locked out.

It were a bad time to strike: no strike fund,
and unions hadn't then the clout
to take the bosses on. No relief
from the Poor Law: the Guardians said
the strikers had refused to work

64

(in our words, they wouldn't scab).
Neighbours did what they could
to help the strikers, but threats –
bailiffs would seize possessions
and folk would lose their homes –
forced Nan's dad an' all back to the mill
on terms worse than they'd had before.

It were different in my day. We sweated
bloody gallons in the foundry's heat
and were always coughing from the dust
hanging in the air. That dust were bad
till the union took the bosses on
and got proper extractor fans put in.
Then, when me lungs were shot
and I needed the extra oxygen,
the union got me compensation – enough
to buy this house halfway up the hill,
closer to the fresher air up top.

Now them folk down there
in the franchises and small businesses,
and all them working zero-hours,
are worse off than ever I were. True,
they don't have to breathe filthy air
like I did ('cept in rush hour,
when that valley's full o' fumes),
but they bloody well need a union,
else what chance will they have
to fight them bosses who're raking it in
for their rights and a decent wage?

He slumps, exhausted:
I wheel him back indoors.
The sun is almost gone.

Flashback

Across the chrome yellow field, the breeze
carries the sweetish smell of urine. Immediately
I'm back in the lab, your incontinence mingling
with the sharp hydrochloric tang as the acid fizzes
on marble chips. A standard experiment, this,
preparing CO_2 to show how the heavy gas
will pour into a jar and snuff a candle out.
Idly, I wonder what happened as you grew up:

did you go to Villa Park, less for the football
than for a rumble with the visiting fans? Now,
sixtyish, you'll be past rumbling, perhaps content
watching matches in the pub with your mates,
arguing over beers till there's no more to be said;
then, staring rheumily into the carbonated head
of your final pint, wondering how long you've got
before the proprietor calls time.

Buttermere, October

Gloom. Grubby wool softly shearing
the Buttermere crags, and the path
to High Stile merely a radius
of circumscribed perception: no prospect
for the camera but the muddy track
and grasses seeded with mist. We descend

a glaciated scour, with no expectation
the sun will break the cloud to rouse
yellowing leaves to a vivid valediction
from spiky branches rendered black.
You tell me yet again to live the present,
not frustrated possibility, and to find delight

in muted hues – the purplish haze
suffusing trees whose sepia trunks
are randomly daubed with lichen's green,
and the lakeside larches' knobbly tan
trailing across the slaty reflection
of Fleetwith Pike. Yet when we return

from transgressing boundaries
to dreary days of domesticity and work,
there'll be no photographic print,
no footmarks fossilised in mud,
no pencilled sketch, nothing
but traces on the palimpsest of mind.

Autumn Retreat

Hand in hand we take the usual path, smooth
and slippery after rain, to the postcard crag.
Grey billows are racing past us, whose blue
interstices let the sun brighten momentarily
a sliver of lime on Causey Pike and burnish
the dull bronze ring of Derwentwater's oak.
We'd hoped for more: Keswick's market
had opened under blue sufficient to preserve
the modesty of a million Dutch and, beyond,
Skiddaw was at last unmasked. Yesterday
the fierce gusts hissing in Rossett's grass
had battered us with cold, slinging mist
low across the pikes. We saw no distant peak,
no point in going on: pleasure could only lie
much closer to – a leafless rowan in the ghyll,
with scarlet bunches swaying above the fall's
impasto black, white and licheny grey;
the yellowy-green of a sheltered ash;
bread, cheese and a hot drink beside the car;
then bath and bed. Today the squalls
are ripping leaves from their failing hold,
virga is veiling Borrowdale, and Castle Crag
is almost gone. No sense in staying out:
we head back to the town and the warmth
of whisky in the bar of The Dog & Gun.

Memento

Orange of grasses, and sedges'
dun seedheads glistening
with light condensed from the sky.
Their vibrancy, catching my eye

on the rise from Duddon Bridge
to Wrynose, pressed the evening
back towards the cypress-green
plantation's edge. I stopped

and squelched across marsh
to kneel, muddily, and marvel
at the dull landscape's brilliance,
inverted, in a myriad of drops.

I picked a head, showering jewels
into the pitch black, sodden peat,
intending to press it between pages –
a memento of our weekend break.

This sedge now lies beneath the maps
and guidebooks in the door pocket,
merely a drab, desiccated memory
slowly decomposing into dust.

Meditation: The South West Coast Path, Cornwall

Cloud shears the tussocky heather moor;
Gurnard's Head butts into a pewter sea;
a pencil of sun momentarily highlights
an ochery arc between grey promontories;
granite stegosaurs relax in rough grass.
Closer to, foxglove, bluebell, trefoil, vetch,
sea carrot and campion compete for bees;
beetles, iridescent green, tussle for nectar
on the orange of a daisy's Colosseum;
six-spot burnets cling *in flagrante* on a stalk.

The footpath descends from cliff-top contour
to brownish boulders crowding the sea's edge
like walrus on a shore. Age has sapped her
energy now: it's a struggle up a tumble of rocks
to regain lost height. Exhausted, she rests,
looking past a glissade dotted with orchids
to flat slabs rebuffing the advances of the sea
and, beyond brackeny steeps, the boats scribing
fleeting collinearities as they ferry tourists
to photograph The Carracks' colony of seals.

Images and notes record particularities
she knows she'll recall imperfectly – the gnarl
of an ivy'd post salvaged from railway junk,
the painted lady spreadeagled on a head
of scabious, the faked stone ring – Medusa's
retribution for the Merry Harvesters' dance.
She'll remember well the qualities – the breeze
on her face; the path's stoniness; the saturating
of colours as the cloud dispersed; the joyous
hours of walking, free from the carer's leash.

The children will scroll through her images,
recalling, with the fuzziness of the nth copy
of a photocopy, her delight in landscapes
and nature's variety of growth and form.
They'll be drawn more to older photographs
made digital from dusty, deteriorating
gelatine – childhoods; rabbits, cats and hamsters;
seaside holidays; teenage self-consciousness;
and family gatherings before the nest, empty,
decomposed into a scatter of fallen twigs.

There's no law of conservation of memory
as there is for energy. She can only record
her experiences in images and words,
always hoping to retain their essences
even though exactness has quickly slithered
from her grasp. She knows her recollections
will, when she has succumbed to the inevitable
entropy of fire, decay till they are undetectable,
like the wake from a tourist boat, forever lost
to the ceaseless restlessness of the sea.

The Carracks are rocky islets off the Cornish coast, between Zennor
and St Ives.

The Merry Harvesters represented by this seemingly ancient
monument on the cliff to the west of Pen Enys Point were apparently
thirteen old farmers and a young woman who were turned to stone for
engaging in a fertility dance on a feast day.

Isolation: A Drama in Five Scenes

Scene 1: Europe, 450 million years ago

No one can tell.
No one was there.
The hominins had gone,
frozen out
by a slow encroachment of ice.

We imagine icy water
from the long-dammed lake
spouting over the ridge,
its stony teeth rasping a channel
through unresisting chalk.

Scene 2: Europe, 180 million years ago

The ice has gone. For the moment,
Neanderthals live on alluvium
deposited by great rivers
flowing from the south and west.

But the ice is creeping back,
driving the Neanderthals away
and damming anew the North Sea
till its waters breach the soft silt
to gouge again.

Scene 3: Europe, 125 million years ago

Warm, very warm. Lush vegetation
borders the Thames' wide estuary.
Hippos are wallowing in the swamps.
No humans have returned:

they, like their forebears, have survived
far from the cold. They scrabble
for clams and crabs on the foreshore,
now and then glancing north
towards white cliffs they know are there
but cannot reach.

Scene 4: Doggerland, 8200 years ago

A low-lying land pockmarked
with lagoons. Men are fishing
from dugouts, unaware

a hundred and eighty miles
of Norway's continental shelf,
far to the north, have collapsed
and a long, low, unstoppable
darkness is coming to sluice away
the people, their huts, their land.

Scene 5: Birling Gap, Sussex, 2019

A century ago photographs showed
coastguards' cottages
set well back from the cliff's edge.

Part of their terrace remains:
scaffolding for the beach steps
has yet again been moved back
to abut the soft coombe rock
that's crumbled faster than the chalk
to either side. Signs warn of the risk
should we approach the brink

and obliquely tell us we must break
the climate's hostile trend
if we're to avoid further retreat,
metre by metre, from the continent
of which we're yet a part.

The Coastguard Cottages, Cuckmere Haven

A saunter along the riverside path, for once free
from the carer's leash. No organising her daily needs,
no cooking, no washing, no calls to bring a drink upstairs,
no interrupted thought, no hurry – a day to delight in
colours: common blues flittering round ragwort heads;
mauve sloes half-hidden in the hedge; blackberries'
tight-clenched maroon; hawthorn berries' arterial red;
heath browns on knapweed; lichen yellowing sapless
trees.

And then a simple pleasure, eating sandwiches
in the August sun, looking at the heritage view –
the cottages slanting across the foreground;
beyond, the Seven Sisters' baleen-like white.

A timeless scene, you'd imagine. Yet without defences,
the cottages' cliff would, in three years, yield a metre –
more if severe storms hit. Below, concrete is holding
against the sea, but all around are reminders
of the sea's relentlessness – dilapidated groynes
angling into the stony beach; shingle scooped away
where waves have burrowed under a wooden palisade;
steel piling rusted to a vivid orange and pierced by sky.

How long can these historic cottages survive?
'Managed retreat' lets them be: for now
it's left to the community to resist
the endless undercutting of the sea.

Dungeness

I walk across alopecic grass half-hiding viper's bugloss,
ragwort and random spiderings of bramble. The horizon,
like a Rothko boundary between tawniness and blue,
is punctuated by two black huts and an abandoned boat.
The larger hut resembles a Grytviken whaling shed:
its roof has collapsed; some wall slats, blown flat,
have exposed a spectrum of plastic crates; and from a nail
a pale blue net spills towards sea-kale's crinkly heads.

Rusted cables and rails lead me from rusted winches
to grey lapstrakes beached beyond the reach of the sea,
like whales hauled ashore to be flensed. Up close, I see
pane-less wheelhouses, lichen's orange on decaying decks,
the hulls' sinewy wood beginning to rot, dabs of blue
clinging to sheerstrakes, and the lapped timbers easing free
from the tight discipline of blue-grey rivets and roves.

Beyond these boats the shingle has been reconfigured,
storm by storm, into furrows deep enough to conceal a man.
I scrunch along the last ridge of this ever-shifting coast,
away from the lighthouses and the blocks of Dungeness B,
captivated by the waves angling in and swooshing
ermine-trimmed robes up the beach whilst surreptitiously
easing its pebbles to the east. Behind me, the breakers
are scrabbling at the power station's shored-up motte,
biding their time till the reactor's life-support is turned off,
the buildings are dismantled block by block, and the motte
is finally abandoned to the relentlessness of their assault.

Bubble

Rush hour. Fumes
drift into the yard
behind the house.

She coughs, hawks
black-specked phlegm
into a tissue.

Her daughter insists
she'll blow a bubble
as big as the world.

She takes a deep breath,
blows steadily
into the viscous film:

the bubble swells slowly
from the wand,
wobbles away.

Dark spots mar
its iridescence.
The world goes pop.

Time Capsule

A piece of piping from a ship?
A bomb?
Or someone's ashes in a tube,
as might be inferred
from the engraved date
and Russian script?
None of these.
Translation reveals it's a time capsule
deposited in the Arctic ice
two years ago:
inside are artefacts of the time –
a menu, wine corks, beer mats,
badges, photographs,
letters and poems –
expected to lie in the ice
for thirty years or more.
And yet here it is in 2020 –
trivial history
fetched up on a Donegal shore,
having floated
more than two thousand miles
after its floe,
perhaps calved from a Greenland glacier,
melted into the sea.

Ice-caps are structured repositories –
layer upon layer of compressed snow
containing dust, isotopes,
inclusions of atmospheric gas
that record the planet's history
long before our time.
But Earth's long-locked history
is melting into amorphousness,
and we are sanderlings –
this foreshore's transient inhabitants –
scurrying along the tideline, searching
for worms, molluscs and crustaceans,
knowing there's not much time
till our shrinking sand bar
yields to the remorselessness
of the sea.

Corridors

Dressed in sisterly blue she sits
at the reception desk, her smile
welcoming you to the atrium
and a choice of openings beyond.

Automatic doors invite you down
a bright-lit corridor – walls sky-blue,
floor beige, ceiling an Arctic white.
Behind you, the doors click shut.

It's as if you'd entered the outcome
of an exercise in perspective,
walls, floor and ceiling converging
on a vanishing-point. At the end

you face another choice,
left or right, but you can't tell
which to take. You choose right:
automatic doors slowly open

into a further corridor similar
to the one you've left, though
this corridor is dingy – the sky-blue
of the walls greyish like smoggy air,

and the ceiling more like snow
concentrating diesel-soot
as it shrinks into the earth.
You make your choice: again,

the doors behind click shut.
There's no handle to the doors,
and you realise you are trapped,
barred from ever going back.

All you can do is walk down
the corridor and choose once more:
yet again you hear the doors click
behind, and know you must go on

down a gloomier corridor littered
with plastic bottles, coffee cups
and bags. Water is dripping
from the ceiling, and black mould

has colonised the walls.
A dim red glow draws you on,
becoming a grimy EXIT sign
above grime-encrusted doors

which begin to open: suddenly
you are afraid, very afraid.

Lendbreen

Cairns are emerging from the ice, one by one:
the pass is yielding to us
clothing, reindeer pelts, leather shoes
and feathered arrows
a thousand or so years old. Higher passes still
grip their ice, their histories
(unlike the climate's trend) yet to be disclosed.

Silver Lining?

The Earth's far hotter than ever we've seen:
with high CO_2, what *quid* for the *quo*?
Soon mangoes will ripen – in Aberdeen.

Glaciers are shrinking, permafrost's melting,
ice-caps are thinning: together they show
the Earth's far hotter than ever we've seen.

You worry malaria will burst on the scene
like Lyme caught from ticks. Don't up sticks and go:
soon melons will ripen – in Aberdeen.

Towns keep flooding after monsoon-like rain.
We don't need measures – we already know
the Earth's far hotter than ever we've seen.

We burn fossil fuels and fracking's not green:
for decades ahead you'll reap what we sow.
Soon lemons will ripen – in Aberdeen.

We've tempo-boosted the Anthropocene
(it's *presto* now, not *adagio*), so
the Earth's far hotter than ever we've seen.
Soon uglies will ripen – in Aberdeen.

The ugli (fruit) is a hybrid of grapefruit, orange and tangerine,
originating in Jamaica.

83

The Lighthouse

The sea is far out,
the sand smooth, unpeopled
by heavy rain.
The overcast breaks:
the lighthouse,
suddenly lit by the sun,
is a brilliant white pinnacle
against the dark base
of a white thundercloud
that's thrusting higher
into the uncurtained blue.

You imagine walking there
(as when you believed
that shining city on the hill
was within your reach)
but the tide is turning,
the clouds are merging,
and all the brilliance
has gone.

Aldeburgh Seascapes

After 'Four Sea Interludes' from 'Peter Grimes' by Benjamin Britten.

Looking at the paintings, I imagine
buffeting north-easterlies whipping
spume from glaucous crests, the plunging
crump of waves, and the hissy rattling
as the camouflaged sea sucks back
through the teeth of shingle shores.

From a bench, I watch the sparse visitors
shuffling around the dim gallery, quietly
contemplating the stilled commotion,
their silhouettes caught for a moment
in the same frame of time. Though I share
the artist's fascination with the sea –

its ebb and flow, its ferociousness and calm,
the ever-changing reflections of the sky –
I'm disappointed. The seascapes here
are too alike, save for one whose glints,
crimson and bloody, are the first hints
of a greater violence that is set to come.

The Scream

After the version Edvard Munch painted in 1910

We know it well –
a sunset of bloody meat,
a black boat, figures
by railings and, facing east,
Munch screaming
at the inevitability of night.

Munch didn't know
his yellow was inferior –
cadmium sulphide
whose chloride contamination
is hygroscopic,
turning yellow to a dirty white.

Dampness has diminished
the vividness of Munch's angst,
but his scream, exposed
to moisture from exhalations,
depicts impermanence –
a slant reminder of what awaits.

Sibelius' Seventh

Sonorous and slow, the symphony unfolds,
the trombone theme a solemn proclamation
of culmination and the barrenness to come.
Eyes brimming, I pull on to the verge and stop.

Depression's nimbus is hanging low, trailing
rain across a rusty heather-softened moor
whose hummocks are jumbled like the crossed
corrugations of a purposeless sea.

Ahead, rippling black in the streaming screen,
is Stanage Edge – a silhouette looming
through the gloom, its fissured face
a huge stone wave forever poised to break.

After completing his seventh symphony in 1924 Sibelius found himself
unable to compose major works during the final thirty years of his life.

Ecology Lesson, Inis Mór

No trees, no houses. Only drystone walls
offer shelter from a northerly wind
that even in cloudless May slices keen
as a whetted blade. Plants dare not stretch far

above the poor soil in the limestone's grykes –
holly and haw merely grow like bonsai
from the darkness, their tiny branches tight
against the grey fossiliferous clints.

Ivy takes less risk, zigzagging its stems
along the cross-cuts and holding its leaves
lightwards, protected from the rip of gales.

Crouched on this wind-scoured flat, I am learning
from these stunted plants how to hunker down
in the darkness of a cleft, and survive.

Llyn Ogwen

Smooth as obsidian
the lake
spreads before me,
a corrie bowl
brimful of night.
Skittering light tracks
across the darkness
to its vanishing-point:

your pebble sinks
towards the sediment.
Dawn-pink arcs disturb
the surface, widening,
overlapping, till calm
returns and offers me
another sunrise,
another world.

Acknowledgements

The following poems were first published as listed below, some in an earlier form.

'Betrayal': *Penumbra*
'Reflections: The Vietnam Veterans' Memorial, Washington DC':
    first place, WAX Arts Socially Engaged Poetry Contest #1
'Bloody Monday, Derry': *Scarlet Leaf* ezine
'War Game': *Pendle War Poetry Anthology*
'Tommy at Seventy': third prize, Sydenham Arts Poetry Competition
'Resurrection: the Sandham Memorial Chapel, Burghclere': in
    An Outbreak of Peace, Arachne Press
'Poppies': *Brain of Forgetting, issue 3* (under the title 'Survivors')
'At the Cenotaph, London': *Silkworm*
'Hawthorns, Wastwater': *Saleopot Magazine*
'Khao Lak, Thailand, Boxing Day 2004': *The Elements* anthology,
    Robin Barratt
'River Wye, Monsal Dale': *Skylark Review*, Little Lantern Press
'At the Hospice Window': *The Writers' Café* ezine
'Shuffling Homeward': *Open Mouse* ezine
'The Scattering': *Saleopot Magazine*
'Arnside Knott': *Allegro*
'Ascension Day': *Nuclear Impact: Broken Atoms in Our Hands* (anthology),
    Shabda Press
'Critical Incident, 21 May 1946': *100 Lives* anthology, Pure Slush
'Fallout': winner, WAX Arts Socially Engaged Poetry Contest #3
'Dreamcatcher': *Bunbury Magazine, issue 17*
'The Blossoming, Kopelovo, 1986': *The Four Seasons* anthology,
    Kind of a Hurricane Press
'Muslyumovo': *DASH*
'Incineration': *AntiHeroin Chic* ezine
'Climbing the Cuillin Ridge': *Brain of Forgetting, issue 3*
'Bray Head': *Cha: An Asian Literary Journal*
'Revelation, Church of St Mary the Virgin, Capel-y-ffin': *Silkworm*
'Graveyard, Church of St Mary the Virgin, Capel-y-ffin:' *Lunar Poetry*
'Quadratura, Sant'Ignazio, Rome': *The Ekphrastic Review*

'Regeneration': *Lunar Poetry*
'Flashback': *Prole*
'Buttermere, October': third prize, Saleopot Members competition
'Autumn Retreat': *The Blue Nib*
'The Coastguard Cottages, Cuckmere Haven': *Mason Street e-journal*
'Lendbreen': highly commended, Micropoem20 competition,
        Centre for New Writing website, University of Manchester
'Silver Lining?': *Earth, We are Listening: An Anthology of Eco-Poetry*,
        Slice of the Moon Books
'Sibelius' Seventh': runner up, Bridgewater Hall poetry competition
'Llyn Ogwen': *Latchkey Tales (Clockwise: The Rising Dawn)*

Mantz Yorke trained as a scientist, gaining a degree in industrial metallurgy before taking up a career in education. He taught in schools and university before becoming an educational researcher. Now retired, he has been able to spend more time writing poetry that reflects his interest in science and human behaviour as well as his enjoyment of, and concern for, the natural environment.

His poems have won prizes and have appeared in print magazines, anthologies and e-magazines in the UK, Ireland, The Netherlands, Israel, Canada, the US, Australia and Hong Kong. His previous collection 'Voyager' is also published by Dempsey & Windle.